5TH GRADE AMERICAN HISTORY: AMERICAN PRESIDENTS

Speedy Publishing LLC
40 E. Main St. #1156
Newark, DE 19711
www.speedypublishing.com

Copyright 2015

All Rights reserved. No part of this book may be reproduced or used in any way or form or by any means whether electronic or mechanical, this means that you cannot record or photocopy any material ideas or tips that are provided in this book

BARACK OBAMA

is the 44th and current President of the United States, and the first African American to hold the office.

GEORGE W. BUSH

was the 43rd President of the United States from 2001 to 2009. He is the eldest son of George H. W. Bush.

BILL CLINTON

was the 42nd President of the United States from 1993 to 2001. He was the third-youngest president.

GEORGE H. W. BUSH

was the 41st President of the United States from 1989 to 1993. He is the second U.S. president to be the father of a U.S. president.

RONALD REAGAN

was the 40th President of the United States from 1981 to 1989. He also served as the 33rd Governor of California from 1967 to 1975.

JIMMY CARTER

was the 39th President of the United States from 1977 to 1981. He was a speed reader and could read up to 2000 words per minute.

GERALD FORD

was the 38th President of the United States, serving from 1974 to 1977. He served as a congressman for 25 years.

LYNDON B. JOHNSON

was the 36th President of the United States from 1963–1969. yndon grew up in a farmhouse in the hill country near Johnson City, Texas.

JOHN F. KENNEDY

was the 35th President of the United States from January 1961 until his assassination in November 1963.

DWIGHT D. EISENHOWER

was the 34th President of the United States from 1953 until 1961. He was a five-star general in the United States Army during World War II.

HARRY S. TRUMAN

was the 33rd President of the United States from 1945 to 1953. He was the only president in the 1900s who did not attend college.

FRANKLIN D. ROOSEVELT

was the 32nd President of the United States from 1933 to 1945. Roosevelt was elected to president for four terms.

CALVIN COOLIDGE

was the 30th President of the United States from 1923 to 1929. He is the only president to be born on Independence Day.

WARREN G. HARDING

was the 29th President of the United States from 1921 to 1923. He was the first president to talk on the radio.

WOODROW WILSON

was the 28th President of the United States, from 1913 to 1921. He was the first president to visit Europe while still in office.

WILLIAM HOWARD TAFT

was the 27th President of the United States, from 1909 to 1913. At 332 pounds, Taft was the heaviest president in history.

THEODORE ROOSEVELT

was the 26th President of the United States, from 1901 to 1909. He was blind in his left eye due to an injury in a boxing match.

BENJAMIN HARRISON

was the 23rd President of the United States, from 1889 to 1893. He was the first president to have electricity in the White House.

GROVER CLEVELAND

was the 22nd and 24th President of the United States, from 1885 to 1889 and 1893 to 1897.

CHESTER A. ARTHUR

was the 21st President of the United States, from 1881 to 1885. One of his favorite hobbies was fishing and he was an excellent fisherman.

JAMES A. GARFIELD

was the 20th President of the United States, serving from March 4, 1881 until his assassination later that year.

RUTHERFORD B. HAYES

was the 19th President of the United States, from 1877 to 1881. He held the first Easter Egg Roll at the White House.

ANDREW JOHNSON

was the 17th President of the United States, serving from 1865 to 1869. Johnson had much of the U.S. Constitution memorized.

ABRAHAM LINCOLN

was the 16th President of the United States, from 1861 to 1865. Lincoln led the United States through its Civil War.

JAMES BUCHANAN

was the 15th President of the United States, from 1857 to 1861. He was once offered a seat on the Supreme Court.

FRANKLIN PIERCE

was the 14th President of the United States, from 1853 to 1857 He had no middle name.

MILLARD FILLMORE

was the 13th President of the United States, from 1850 to 1853. He opposed President Abraham Lincoln during the Civil War.

ZACHARY TAYLOR

was the 12th President of the United States, from 1849 to 1850. Taylor died suddenly of a stomach-related illness in July 1850.

JAMES K. POLK

was the 11th President of the United States, from 1845 to 1849. Polk was the first president to have his photograph taken while in office.

JOHN TYLER

was the 10th President of the United States, from 1841 to 1845. With his two wives he fathered 15 children, more than any other president.

WILLIAM HENRY HARRISON

was the 9th President of the United States (1841). He was also the first president to die in office.

MARTIN VAN BUREN

was the 8th President of the United States, from 1837 to 1841. He was the first president to be born as a citizen of the United States.

ANDREW JACKSON

was the 7th President of the United States, from 1829 to 1837. Jackson is the only president to have been a prisoner of war.

JAMES MONROE

was the 5th President of the United States, from 1817 to 1825. He was the third president to die on the 4th of July.

JAMES MADISON

was the 4th President of the United States, from 1809 to 1817. He was 5 feet 4 inches tall and weighed 100 pounds.

THOMAS JEFFERSON

was the 3rd President of the United States, from 1801 to 1809. Jefferson was also an accomplished architect.

JOHN ADAMS

was the 2nd President of the United States, from 1797 to 1801. Adams was the first president to live in the White House.

GEORGE WASHINGTON

was the 1st President of the United States, from 1789 to 1797. He was the only president unanimously elected.